*Young America*
*in the "Now" World*

THE CHARLES C. MOSKOWITZ LECTURES     NUMBER XII

Charles C. Moskowitz, Senator Hubert H. Humphrey, and Dean Abraham L. Gitlow assembled on the occasion of Senator Humphrey's delivery of the C. C. Moskowitz lecture.

# *Young America in the "Now" World*

## Hubert H. Humphrey

THE CHARLES C. MOSKOWITZ LECTURES
SCHOOL OF COMMERCE
NEW YORK UNIVERSITY

NEW YORK   *New York University Press*   1971

# FOREWORD

THE CHARLES C. MOSKOWITZ LECTURES are arranged by the School of Commerce of New York University and aim at advancing public understanding of the issues that are of major concern to business and the nation. Established through the generosity of Mr. Charles C. Moskowitz, a distinguished alumnus of the School of Commerce and formerly Vice-President-Treasurer and a Director of Loew's Inc., they have enabled the School to make a significant contribution to public discussion and understanding of important issues affecting the American economy and its business enterprise.

The present lecture is somewhat special and apart from the regular series, differing in format as well as in thrust. Where recent lectures involved several speakers and a panel of discussants, this one presented a single lecturer. And where past lec-

7

tures in the series related rather immediately to business and the economy, this one assumed a broader scope and considered "The 'Now Generation' and Society Tomorrow." The present lecture is special also in the rather unique background and range of life experience possessed by the lecturer, for Senator Hubert H. Humphrey combines qualities of intellectuality and public service which are extraordinary. Having narrowly missed election to the Presidency in 1968, he spent two years as Distinguished Professor of Political Science at Macalester College and Professor of Social Sciences at the University of Minnesota. But the beginning of 1971 saw his return to the Senate in which he had earlier served some two decades and over which he had presided as Vice President of the United States in the hectic years between 1964 and 1968.

Observing that "the past is prologue," Senator Humphrey invited the attention of the "Now Generation" to the arena of world affairs—and to a consideration of how the "Then Generation" of its parents had gotten the United States so deeply and so sweepingly involved in the international sphere. He pointed out that America's internationalism of the post World War II years was a reaction to America's isolationism of the years between the two great conflagrations, and, more fundamentally, to the realization that isolationism had, in itself, contributed to the growth of dictatorships in the interwar period and, finally, to the horror that lasted from 1939 to 1945.

Nineteen Forty-Five! As one of the "Then Generation," I remember it well, especially its historic highpoints: V-E Day, which I celebrated on the remote island of Biak in the South Pacific; and V-J Day, which found me in the Philippines. Happy days for us. "Euphoric" is the word Senator Humphrey used to describe the mood of the movement in the allied nations. We really did think that peace would prevail.

The dream faded so fast. The cleavage between the Soviet Union and the United States became clear so quickly and so starkly, as did our resolve to be involved, not to turn our backs on Europe and the rest of the world which so desperately needed our aid. In Senator Humphrey's words: ". . . we overreacted in a real sense. We were determined to hold off the return of isolation, and we worked diligently to build structures of collective security that would bring order out of near chaos. The words 'collective security' were almost magic whenever there was a problem."

"The massive effort took us suddenly into a new and often confusing era in our history. We abandoned almost overnight the most basic tenet of our historic foreign policy to 'beware of entangling alliances'."

In "an instant of time in man's history," we

moved from isolationism to massive internationalism, from a provincial state to a superpower. We stood against naked aggression in Korea and fought for stability in international affairs, and almost unwittingly found ourselves finally in a distant, strange, and cruel war in Vietnam.

That war has brought America disillusionment, disenchantment, and discord. But it has brought also another fundamental moment of decision to our nation, for many Americans today seem, once again, to turn to isolationism and a rejection of all United States overseas involvements. And it is a moment of decision of particular importance to our youth, to the "Now Generation." Its elders, in the name of idealism and out of a realization of the oneness of the world, as well as out of first-hand experience with the failure of isolationism, took to involvement—to internationalism. That turn yielded the Marshall Plan, the Truman Doctrine, and massive programs for foreign aid. It yielded also Vietnam. Because of the last, will our youth turn back to isolationism?

Senator Humphrey hoped it would not. He said it was necessary for us to reassess our role internationally and at home, to avoid deep involvements abroad which affect our national interests only slightly, and to concentrate far more heavily on our domestic difficulties. But he argued against a return to isolationism. He argued that we must build a just and humane social structure at home, but he argued just as strongly that it would be dangerous and absurd for us to abandon Europe, the Middle East, and the rest of the world. And it would be impossible for us to isolate ourselves, because the facts of technology, trade, transport, and travel have really ruled it out.

With such logic, Senator Humphrey called for a positive and enlightened American involvement in the world, an involvement which, while not sapping our ability to address ourselves meaningfully to our domestic problems, would enable us to pursue these objectives: (1) an emphasis on ideas, resources, and experience in our aid to other nations, rather than an emphasis on military power; (2) a concentration on preserving our planet from the threat of nuclear war; (3) a stubborn and persevering effort to achieve a common understanding with the Soviet Union, for without that the danger of a nuclear holocaust is ever present; (4) a major and continuing effort to end the isolation of China and to bring her into the community of nations; (5) a massive educational undertaking with the objective of increasing and broadening the knowledge and understanding of Americans relative to Oriental and other peoples of different cultures; and (6) a deliberate insistence that Asian nations themselves assume primary responsibility for their own security and development, with a view to encouraging such important Asian nations as Japan and India to assume a greater leadership role.

Beyond the foregoing, Senator Humphrey pointed out a central dilemma in foreign policy; "the difficulty of reconciling stability with change." But he thought we could manage that, providing we were ready ourselves to accept significant change.

He spoke of Europe and our involvement there as an example. Unlike Asia, which he felt not to be vital, he saw Europe as critical to us, and stated flatly that we are a European power. Therefore, we must not disengage ourselves from Europe precipitously or unilaterally. Instead, we must work carefully and in partnership with our European allies to bring the continent to a viable, if not an altogether harmonious, peace. In that way, we will hopefully find our way to troop reductions and an ultimate détente between Eastern and Western Europe. And change will have been accomplished along with stability.

Finally, and with some passion, Senator Humphrey called out to the "Now Generation" to realize that the search for peace is much more than withdrawing from Vietnam, that it is the development of life, the enrichment of life. And development means involvement internationally and sharing some of our wealth with others. However, the Senator believes that our efforts in this connection must be multilateral, must work through such institutions as the U. N. and the World Bank. He reiterated specifically and strongly that international peace-keeping must go on, because there are threats to the peace which will not go away simply because the United States quits the international arena. Therefore, we must not quit. Rather, we must work toward the building of a workable international system of peace-keeping.

These are some of the fundamental challenges facing the "Now Generation." How it meets them will determine how history will judge it—when it has become the "Then Generation." Senator Humphrey does not think it will fail, nor does he think the generation of its parents failed. And with this note of uplift rather than of scolding, he concluded his lecture and received the applause of his audience.

Abraham L. Gitlow
Dean

THE CHARLES C. MOSKOWITZ LECTURES were established through the generosity of a distinguished alumnus of the School of Commerce, Mr. Charles C. Moskowitz of the Class of 1914, who retired after many years as Vice President-Treasurer and a Director of Loew's, Inc.

In establishing these lectures, it was Mr. Moskowitz's aim to contribute to the understanding of the function of business and its underlying disciplines in society by providing a public forum for the dissemination of enlightened business theories and practices.

The School of Commerce and New York University are deeply grateful to Mr. Moskowitz for his continued interest in, and contribution to, the educational and public service program of his alma mater.

This volume is the twelfth in the Moskowitz series. The earlier ones were:

February, 1961   *Business Survival in the Sixties*
*Thomas F. Patton*, President and
Chief Executive Officer
Republic Steel Corporation

November, 1961   *The Challenges Facing Management*
*Don G. Mitchell*, President
General Telephone and Electronics
Corporation

November, 1962   *Competitive    Private    Enterprise
Under Government Regulation*
*Malcolm A. MacIntyre*, President
Eastern Air Lines

November, 1963   *The Common Market: Friend or
Competitor?*
*Jesse W. Markham*, Professor of
Economics, Princeton University
*Charles E. Fiero*, Vice President,
The Chase Manhattan Bank
*Howard S. Piquet*, Senior Specialist
in International Economics, Legislative Reference Service, The
Library of Congress

November, 1964   *The Forces Influencing the American Economy*
*Jules Backman*, Research Professor
of Economics, New York University

*Martin R. Gainsbrugh*, Chief Economist and Vice President, National Industrial Conference Board

November, 1965 *The American Market of the Future*
*Arno H. Johnson*, Vice President
and Senior Economist, J. Walter
Thompson Company
*Gilbert E. Jones*, President, IBM
World Trade Corporation
*Darrell B. Lucas*, Professor of Mar-
keting and Chairman of the De-
partment, New York University

November, 1966 *Government Wage-Price Guide-*
*posts in the American Economy*
*George Meany*, President, Ameri-
can Federation of Labor and
Congress of Industrial Organi-
zations
*Roger M. Blough*, Chairman of the
Board and Chief Executive Offi-
cer, United States Steel Corpora-
tion
*Neil H. Jacoby*, Dean, Graduate
School of Business Administra-
tion, University of California at
Los Angeles

November, 1967 *The Defense Sector in the Ameri-*
*can Economy*

*Jacob K. Javits,* United States Senator, New York

*Charles J. Hitch,* President, University of California

*Arthur F. Burns,* Chairman, Federal Reserve Board

November, 1968 *The Urban Environment: How It Can Be Improved*

*William E. Zisch,* Vice-chairman of the Board, Aerojet-General Corporation

*Paul H. Douglas,* Chairman, National Commission on Urban Problems

Professor of Economics, New School for Social Research

*Robert C. Weaver,* President, Bernard M. Baruch College of the City University of New York

Former Secretary of Housing and Urban Development

November, 1969 *Inflation: The Problems It Creates and the Policies It Requires*

*Arthur M. Okun,* Senior Fellow, The Brookings Institution

*Henry H. Fowler,* General Partner, Goldman, Sachs & Co.

*Milton Gilbert,* Economic Adviser, Bank for International Settlements

March, 1971     *The Economics of Pollution*

*Kenneth E. Boulding,* Professor of
Economics, University of Colo-
rado

*Elvis J. Stahr,* President, National
Audubon Society

*Solomon Fabricant,* Professor of
Economics, New York University
Former Director, National Bureau
of Economic Research

*Martin R. Gainsbrugh,* Adjunct
Professor of Economics, New
York University
Chief Economist, National Indus-
trial Conference Board

CONTENTS

# YOUNG AMERICA
# IN THE "NOW" WORLD

THE "NOW GENERATION" has had its work cut out for it by my generation. The young people of this generation have been living through a whirlwind. The times are wild, and there has been a great deal of tension the "Now Generation" has had to live through. This generation has been subjected to more diverse and rapid physical and psychic stimulation in only five years than my generation was in their first twenty years. Young people must assimilate a world of facts, and learn the lessons of the past. The "Now Generation" may not have readily available the time for reflection. It may not have accessible the kind of atmosphere that is conducive to "Sweet Silent Thought" and the "Remembrance of Things Past." But this generation must find the time for knowledge and a capacity for commitment, while remembering that knowledge without commitment

25

is wasteful, but commitment without knowledge is dangerous.

One lesson young people must learn from the past, that I would like to discuss, is global. It is learning how to achieve peace. And it is a lesson the "Now Generation" must learn quickly and fully, for my generation has learned that war in Vietnam has cost us more than 45,000 American lives and almost 300,000 casualties, more than 115 billion dollars of American wealth, and division and discord at home.

What else have we learned? What lessons have we managed to comprehend as a result of the blood and treasure we have expended on southeast Asia? What will we think and do that will differ from the way we thought and acted a decade ago? These are not simple questions to answer. War has compelled us to reexamine our role in the world, to study in historical perspective what we have done and to make us seek peace and security today and in the future. War has compelled us to reexamine our goals and our priorities, and to examine the means we intend to take to achieve them. But we have no mechanism in this government today to arrive at what we might call a consensus as to what are the goals of our nation or what are the priorities.

Twenty-five years ago, we were nearing the end of a bitter and costly war. And we looked forward hopefully to a new world at peace. We had to learn to achieve amity and cooperation, and strong moral limits on the use of power. That is, we had learned not to repeat the mistake we had made in the 1920s. We resolved to accept the role of international responsibility. We refused to turn our backs on Europe and other parts of the world that needed our help, and we worked diligently to build structures of collective security, underscored by our leadership in creating the United Nations, in forging the NATO Alliance, and in huge investments in foreign aid. Perhaps we overreacted in a real sense, for we abandoned almost overnight the most basic tenet of our historic foreign policy: "beware of entangling alliances." Nevertheless, our commitments today stretch around the world and include alliances with forty-three nations.

The massive effort to help other nations took us suddenly into a new and often confusing era of our history, and no other nation was required to do —and learn—so much in so little time. There was no precedent to follow, but I believe we met the demands placed on us with a surprising degree of sophistication and success. We learned to use our power and generously shared our resources to bring political stability and economic recovery to the nations ravaged by World War II. We learned that we had to provide a shield of protection behind which other peoples and nations could once again stand, strong and renewed. We knew that we must meet the force of aggression, we fought to bring stability in the Middle East [1] as we did in Korea. But we were also extending our power bit by bit into Southeast Asia and we became embroiled in a strange and cruel war that defied all norms of conventional warfare. The war in Vietnam has brought with it such disillusion and discord that many Americans of every political persuasion question anew all of our involvements overseas. There is the growing feeling that we will abandon our role of international involvement. Our allies in Europe especially are concerned, and their fears are fostered by the misguided tendency in the United States to regard all our separate commitments in the world as indivisible —seeing in our efforts to disengage from Vietnam the threat that we will abandon Europe and the Middle East as well. But we must not let our experience in Vietnam lead us to forget the lessons we have learned from the events following World War II and the fact that for twenty-five years we helped preserve the world from a major war, did help this world in many ways, and, especially, averted a nuclear holocaust. We have learned that it is impossible for us to isolate ourselves physically, politically, or economically from the rest of the world. However, we also have learned that we must not become deeply involved where we have little at

1. See Appendix I.

stake, or where our own security can be protected by other means than armed intervention.

We can—and we must—readjust the scale and nature of our involvements, and manage these changes intelligently. But we must be careful not to act in haste, not to effect a short-sighted and ultimately futile moral disengagement from the world. We have learned that there are equal dangers of overinvolvement and blind abstention. We must carefully steer a course between the two.

We also have learned that we must turn our minds and talents, and direct our resources to pressing needs at home. The traditional line dividing domestic from foreign affairs has become as indistinct as a line drawn through water. This means that our place in the world and the nature of our own society have become indivisible. It is very difficult to talk peace abroad as you wage war at home. It is very difficult to talk about human dignity abroad as you practice bigotry and discrimination and racism at home. It is very difficult for a nation to speak of the hungry throughout the world and close our eyes to the victims of malnutrition in our own midst. The best foreign policy is a good domestic policy. If we are concerned with our own ills, we may very well be able to have real concern for others—at least others may believe us.

Our structure of common defense and security could prove to be only a hard outer shell that could collapse on an empty center unless we bring new strength to areas of our internal life that are threatened on every side—as we see our environment polluted and damaged; our cities rotting; our systems of education and health care grossly inadequate; our people torn by bitter dissention.

We have learned that there are limits to the use of military power, and these limits need to be defined.[2] That is, we have seen in recent years that, while we and the Soviet Union have become more powerful in strictly military terms, our ability to use this power has become more limited; we must not underestimate the latent power and effects of nuclear weapons. They are still of central importance in affecting the relations among the major nations of the world. But, now, at a time of mutual deterrence, their mystique is dwindling. This is due to the fact that we are living in a new age of pluralism. The bonds of alliances are weakening, both in the West and the Communist world; the Sino-Soviet rivalry gives firm evidence that the Communist monolith is no more. Even Soviet military occupation of Czechoslovakia has failed to quash hopeful developments in Eastern Europe. Also, there is a growing division between rich nations and poor, which has little relation to military might. Many new nations from the developing world are becoming involved in world politics, and individual countries are making new

2. See Appendix II.

diplomatic arrangements with little reference to the super powers that once were virtually the sole custodians of security. In today's world, power is proving to be persuasive only to the extent that it is appropriate to local circumstances and the interests of local powers.

The plain fact is that there is a much greater play of other power forces: economic, political, and psychological. Almost everywhere, there is a return to the power of ideas and ideals, and effective action in the world now often means that wealth, talent, and ideals must be applied to international problems—not just by the super powers, but by many nations.

In these changed circumstances, how can we develop a new approach to deal with events? What can our country do to help build peace, stability, and ordered change? To a great extent, as we have seen in the recent past, we must develop new methods and approaches that are rooted less in our military power and more in what we have to offer other nations in the way of ideas, resources, and experience.

But first and foremost, we must help to preserve life from the threat of nuclear war, and this is not simple or preordained. The fact that we have not had a nuclear war for twenty-five years is no assurance that it will not come. We cannot take for granted our survival in a nuclear-powered world, for both the United States and the Soviet Union now have far more power than they need merely to deter one another. This came about because, for nearly twenty years, we have lived with the doctrines of deterrence, based on a healthy distrust for each other. It was, and is, necessary for both Russia and the United States—indeed, for anyone in the world —to survive the nuclear age. Although in the last few years we managed to add a small measure of stability to the mad balance of nuclear armaments, a balance of terror rather than of power, today we are entering a period during which new super weapons are being developed, which will again no longer assure us that there is any balance of power, or that we can deter the Russians, and—as strange as it may seem—they have similar doubts about their ability to deter us. But, even so, the SALT negotiations in Helsinki and Vienna now seem to have come to an impasse. I hope this is not the case and that there will be arrangements forthcoming that will limit both strategic and defensive nuclear systems. There are some hopeful signs. Perhaps the fact that the Russians are reducing the rate at which they are deploying their SS-9 and the obsolete nature of the Moscow ABM or Galosh System would indicate that they desire at least to negotiate in some atmosphere of de-escalation. Perhaps, as well, Congressional limitation of the ABM and the declaration to limit the involvement of United States troops in conflicts abroad indicate that the United States wishes to make agreements of substance and scope.

The fact that the United States has begun to deploy MIRV on both the Poseidon and Minuteman II, and the Soviets are doing much the same, only indicates that negotiators for the United States and Russia must make every effort to reach agreements that are reciprocal. I do not think that we have the luxury of time or opportunity to insist on comprehensive agreement; this would be the ideal. However, we must not decline to accept some agreement, even though agreement to limit all systems cannot be reached.

We have valuable precedents to support Presidential overtures to agree to limit the nuclear arms race. In 1958, President Eisenhower offered to halt American testing of nuclear weapons for a period of one year following the beginning of negotiations for a formal treaty, if the United Kingdom and the Soviet Union would follow suit. This moratorium, taken with no formal agreement at all, lasted for nearly three years. In 1963, President Kennedy again ordered a halt to testing nuclear weapons in the atmosphere and proposed to maintain the ban as long as the Russians did. They agreed and the test ban treaty was signed.

Today, I call on President Nixon to halt deployment of the ABM and delay further deployment of MIRV. We would run no serious risks, for we could always continue our programs if the Russians continued to develop their nuclear weapons. At least we would have tried. And I think that for this "Now

Generation" we have an obligation to try, for they will inherit the vastly accelerated and escalated terror which is in these weapons. We must work patiently with the Soviet Union to achieve one common goal: continued survival in a world where nuclear weapons technology is our greatest enemy. From now on, we must base much of our security on greater political understanding, or we will have no security at all!

I do not argue that we should trust the Russians in all of our dealings with them. We cannot. The Russians still are not prepared to consider agreements with us or with our allies over many matters in which we compete or have conflicts of interest. But, unless we transform Soviet-American relations in the critical area of nuclear weapons, where we can inspect, where technology does permit some security, we may not live to debate other questions of serious but lesser importance.

We will need a new diplomacy, as well as Presidential appeals and SALT negotiations, managed with skill and patience. Taking into full account the interests of our allies, we must seek to turn all aspects of our relations with the Soviet Union from the sterile by-ways of mutual military confrontation into more hopeful paths of political accommodation. We could usefully begin annual meetings at the highest level between American and Russian leaders—not these ambitious, showmanlike, newspaper-headline summit talks that are held once in a while.

We have that obligation to the rest of the world. We also should expand trade relations, cultural contacts and cooperation in the areas of science, commerce and technology.

Our relations with the Soviet Union are of the greatest importance in our concern for the survival of life, but other developments that have taken place in the 1970s are of concern as well. One of the most important of these is the emergence of China as a major power in Asia. Today, the power of China is more of a psychological nature than it is actual. But that power is growing, and it would be a fatal error if we let ignorance and unreasoning fear of the future Chinese military power cause us to close the door to political understandings with Peking. We must do all we can bring China into the community of nations, free from paranoia and committed to respecting the legitimate rights of her neighbors. An isolated China is a threat to all nations. A China that is involved with the outside world will still pose problems, and perhaps even threats of a serious nature, but at least we can sustain the hope that accommodation will replace antagonism.

We must realize that the legacy of embittered Sino-American relations will not be overcome in a year, or perhaps even a decade. But we can do much to come to terms with China. Our initiatives—always taken in full consultation with our allies—should lead to diplomatic recognition of China and admission to the United Nations. We must relax trade and travel restrictions with China. We should encourage cultural exchanges with China, to broaden the contacts between our peoples. All this must be a part of the *new diplomacy.*

The primary responsibility for security and the development of Asia rests with the Asian nations themselves. They must take the lead, for they best understand themselves—their past and their hopes for the future. We ourselves are pathetically weak in knowledge of Asian culture, languages, history, religions, and the people. We should be prepared to cooperate, to be a helpful partner but not a dominating force. That is, we should follow certain guidelines to help the Asians. First, we should establish that the Asian countries are themselves willing to achieve their own security and to undertake their own economic and social development if we are going to help them at all. Second, we should allow the Asian nations themselves as well as regional organizations the primary responsibility to provide their own security and to achieve economic development. Third, we should provide aid carefully and selectively. Our efforts should be justified by our own interests and responsibilities, and they should be concentrated on economic development through multilateral means. Hopeful developments in Asia will be lasting only if they spring from the efforts of the people themselves and only if they command broad local support.

Japan is perhaps the most important nation with

which we should cooperate. She is more than our economic competition; she is the most powerful nation in Asia—not in military terms, but in economic strength. She has no weapons, but the Japanese have a thorough knowledge of the Asian continent, a historical knowledge of its divserse cultures, and they understand the economic and trading patterns. Nor are the Japanese bound by the power politics of the past. These qualities might enhance the opportunity for the Japanese people to play a leading role in Asia, to help it enter a new era of social and economic development.

We have learned from our experience in Southeast Asia that we face a dilemma in our foreign policy: the difficulty of reconciling stability with change. That is, we recognize that we must have stability in our relations with Russia, which is necessary for the survival of the world. But we also recognize that unless there is economic, social, and political change in the world, then stability will prove fruitless and self-defeating.

We have to find ways to promote change within a framework of order, or the future of the world will be marked by anarchy or repression. We can begin by supporting the efforts being made in Europe, for example, to move away from more than twenty years of confrontation toward a European commonwealth. This is beginning to happen. The United States no longer has the dominating voice in European politics, nor should it (although many

Americans think we should because "we rescued them, you know"). The United States, however, is still a European power, and it should remain deeply involved in providing security and confidence, otherwise there would be little or no hope for change.

Would it be wise, therefore, for the United States today abruptly to reduce its commitment to NATO, as some advocate we should? As I see it, I doubt that we will achieve mutual and balanced force reductions if we act alone. We will not convince the Soviet Union to accept rules of civilized behavior in Eastern Europe if we lose interest in European affairs. We will not reassure our allies we are really concerned with their future if we appear to be insensitive to their anxieties and needs. We must show that our partnership with Europe really means something and support efforts to resolve the division of the Continent.

The United States should encourage our allies in their proposal for a European Security Conference, recognizing its limitations, but realizing that this conference could become part of the political process leading to what we all want—troop reductions throughout all Europe. Furthermore, I think we should engage in a constant program of discussions and negotiations on troop reductions at the highest levels. We should encourage political contacts between our allies and the nations of the Warsaw Pact, such as the recent effort by the West German government to improve its relations with the Soviet

Union and the eastern Europeans nations. I believe we should make the NATO alliance more than an instrument of defense, rigidly committed to the past; we should make it an instrument of international peaceful engagement. Working with our allies, we can help liquidate the legacy of military confrontation.

We face the same dilemma in our foreign policy with the rest of the world that we face in Europe. But bringing about orderly change elsewhere in the world will be even more difficult to resolve. There are more than a billion people in the world today in countries where the average per capita income is under one hundred dollars a year. Hundreds of millions live on less than fifty dollars a year. Evidence has shown us that poverty and deprivation, coupled with the beginning of education and hope, can create what we call "the revolution of rising expectations." And I think we know that people all over the world know what modern society can mean for their families. The man in Korea, or Guatamala, or Zambia knows what you and I have. He knows about the vast resources at our command and at the command of other fortunate nations. This awareness helps to widen even further the gaps between "the have" and "the have not" people of the earth. The inequality is polarizing the world into north and south, the rich and the poor, the white and nonwhite. And, I submit, this is a recipe for strife, both between the world's divided halves and throughout the developing world. Pope John said, "Where there is constant want there is no peace."

It is not just getting out of war that makes for peace, because peace is something more than the absence of war. Peace is the development of life, the enrichment of life. There is tragedy today that takes more lives every day because of poverty, malnutrition, and disease than any war. Yet, as we hear the cry for peace, all too few people lift their voices to help. Today, our material contribution to the developing world is less than 1 percent. Many other nations far exceed what we are doing. The search for peace, to put it succinctly, is more than withdrawing from Vietnam. Pope Paul has reminded us that "Development is the new name for peace," and unless we contribute to it, we are not contributing to peace.

Our commitment has to be to nation-building. Our interest should be the creation of nations that are independent and secure, not the purchase of favors in the developed world. To achieve this, I think we must channel our aid through multilateral institutions, the United Nations, the World Bank, and regional organizations established for development of Asia, Africa, and Latin America. This will place heavy demands on these organizations, but this policy will work only if the commitment to non-interference in the internal affairs of other countries is maintained, and the policy is respected by all states large and small. This is only possible if there is an effective instrument in the international community, such as the United Nations, to serve the interests, not of individual states but of peace itself.

Finally, for us to learn what our future role in the world is to be, we need to change many of our basic ideas about the world, and we must learn about other nations, other people, more than we ever have before. For too long our isolation from the rest of the world allowed us to think we were at the center of it. Too often, our schools are so intent on teaching the myths of American destiny that they ignore the billions of people who find us as foreign as we find them. Too often our newspapers and our television only report events in other lands that directly affect us, or translate events into American terms even at the price of gross distortion. For years, we had no information in this country about Latin America, unless there was a coup or revolution. For years we knew nothing about Africa. There weren't half a dozen top reporters in Africa in 1960—until there was a revolution in the Congo.

In the past quarter-century we have followed a foreign policy we formulated for the whole world while we understood the world only in part. We know much about Europe, a little about Asia, and we are almost totally ignorant of the developing areas of the world. There has been, and continues to be this "knowledge gap" that threatens our survival. Yet with a glaring gap in our knowledge of the world we live in, we have made commitments;

and as I have said, commitments without knowledge are dangerous, and can be disastrous. Indeed, would we have ever become involved in Vietnam if we had known more about it?

Like other great nations before us, we have too often suffered from the myopia of power, imputing to others attitudes about the world they do not hold, and, often, in our zeal, imposing our cultural ideas where they are not wanted. Although we see others mimicking our material advances, from the automobile to indoor plumbing, we fail to realize that superiority on the assembly line may not mean superiority in a way of life. And we must realize that other nations are challenged to resist this "American Challenge." This is really a challenge to us. We must break with the tradition that leads great nations to practice cultural imperialism. We must show that we can be involved in the world without trying to dominate it. This does not mean that we must shy away from making available what we have to offer. It is one thing to give freely of what you have; it is quite another thing to demand that our ways prevail.

We have the challenge to know ourselves—what is best in our tradition and what would benefit from an infusion of ideas and the experience of others. This is a challenge to our schools, our universities, and the media to help us to become educated in world citizenship that we need so urgently. Only with a better public understanding of our world can we make it a better world. And we have the challenge to abandon that element of self-righteousness that has stigmatized much of our foreign policy— the tendency to substitute moralisms for morality and legalisms for the rule of law. We need to gain a new perspective on the world, and the history of our involvement in it, seeing ourselves neither as saviors uniquely endowed with good, nor as villains possessed by evil. And we can no longer see the world as divided between friends and enemies. We will benefit no one, least of all ourselves, if we corrupt our view of the world by, and base the resolution of all our dilemmas in foreign policy on, a simple, misleading, and often dangerous choice between right and wrong.

This is the challenge. We must remember that many of the aspirations of other peoples follow a tradition that we ourselves began. But we must find ways of being involved in the world that will protect our security without stifling the legitimate desires of people who strive for their freedom, their identity, and their personal fulfillment. We must learn to seek peace without precluding change. We must learn to be patient and not expect a world to emerge that will be at peace in a day, or even a year, or perhaps even in a decade. And we must learn how we can rely on our ideals once again to guide our involvement, not ignoring the facts of power, but not letting them destroy the human dimensions of our policy. We must place greater emphasis on human and personal values—having enough to eat, being able to learn, living free of fear. I believe we can do it. I believe we can make our ideals powerful again.

I have great faith in the "Now Generation." Faith that, through their ideals and aspirations, they will find the path to peace. I don't think it is wrong to see nations and peoples in terms of the Spirit—of things that are not material. I think that what this nation is longing for, above all, is not just a better economy, but a sense of compassion, of a justice it believes it could have. And I appeal to these hopes and aspirations. I ask our people to believe that what we have learned in this tragedy of war and suffering has made us a wiser people. I am not sure, but I have the right to believe so, and I shall.

# APPENDIX I

ONE OF THE MOST VITAL, if not the most sensitive, issues facing this country is the critical situation in the Mideast.

It is my view that the Mideast is a powder keg with a very short fuse and ready to explode if any one of the participants strikes the match of renewed hostility.

It is, therefore, imperative that every effort be made by this Government and hopefully by the Soviet Union to restrain any action on the part of the Arab States or Israel that might create a situation of war and hostilities again.

I deeply regret that there has not been a renewal of the cease-fire. Even though the situation exists in which there has been no combat, the renewal of the cease-fire would be much more reassuring.

I would note in this instance that the State of

Israel was prepared for that renewal under the terms of the United Nations resolution, but the United Arab Republic rejected it.

The Senator from Washington clearly defined the interest of this Nation in the Mideast. It is not just Israel and the Arab States. It is the United States and her relations with the Soviet Union. It is a matter of our own national security as well as whatever our interests may be in the neighboring countries of that area.

The Senator has made it very clear that the Soviet Union, while not wanting an all-out war, does not want an all-out peace. He has pointed out the importance to the Soviets of a policy of maintaining a degree of tension in the Mideast.

Let me say as one who has had the opportunity of studying this question both in and out of this body and as one who has had the opportunity of visiting on this matter with the Chairman of the Secretariat Council of the Soviet Union that the Soviet Union does want Israel to withdraw back to the armistice line, a situation which existed prior to the 6-Day War in 1967. That is their policy. That is what they are talking about now.

I am afraid that the Government of the United States is going to be a party to that policy which will make it very difficult, if not impossible, to arrive at what the other part of the United Nations resolution provides—secure and recognized boundaries.

It would be the height of folly on the part of this Nation if we did not insist upon negotiations, and I mean negotiations that would be in an atmosphere containing the possibility of some results.

If Israel withdraws prior to those negotiations, she will have lost any bargaining power she may have. To accept withdrawal as a matter of principle is not the problem. That has been accepted in the United Nations resolution. And all arguments to the contrary, what is now accepted in all chanceries of the world as the U.S. position is that Israel should withdraw and that after that we will do our level best to make sure that she have protection and guarantees. Those protections and guarantees to Israel are a matter of history.

I was in the United Nations as a delegate from this body in 1966. I heard Golda Meir, Foreign Minister at that time, speak to the United Nations. Under pressure of the United States for total withdrawal, Israel withdrew. We gave guarantees. There was a United Nations peace force. In 1967 Nasser told the peace force to get out. The United Nations Secretary General withdrew the peace force and war was inevitable.

What Israel is asking for today is in our national interest. If we let this situation of 1966-67 develop again, her boundaries will not be secure and recognized. It will precipitate a horrible possibility of confrontation in the Mideast once again between the United States and the Soviet Union.

Our foreign policy should be one of trying to readjust Israel's frontiers so that there should not be any need for American forces.

The argument has been made here by the Senators from New York, Washington, and Connecticut that it is in the national interest of this country. It is not related directly to only the well-being of Israel. Above all, every Member of the Senate knows that the Mediterranean is part of the underbelly of NATO, to which we have commitments. The Soviet Union has penetrated into that area, primarily the Middle East, far beyond its wildest dreams. What Catherine the Great failed to do, Kosygin and Brezhnev will have succeeded in doing.

If we permit Soviet forces to remain in Egypt, we will have a situation in which we have Soviet forces legitimatized under the United Nations resolution. It will only increase the tension and provide an excuse for the Soviet presence far beyond the United Nations force.

I want to add this word about the President. Every decision relating to the Mideast has ultimately been made by the President. For some reason the State Department gets befuddled and confused on this issue. President Nixon has kept the options open. He has been eminently fair. He has done many good things. We owe him a great deal of respect and, indeed, of praise for what he has done this far.

I urge the President not to permit other officers of Government to bind his hands. The President can use the force of his office and the prestige of his office, not to dominate but to encourage negotiations, and that is what is needed.

The United States and the Soviet Union must recognize their international obligations by exercising restraint on those countries party to the present conflict in the Middle East.

We should keep our sights on diplomacy and negotiation, the only way to peaceful settlement.

I propose that the United States make a supreme effort so that the parties to the conflict will:

First, renew the cease-fire.

Second, continue active support of and participation in the work of the Jarring mission.

Third, present their respective proposals for a peaceful settlement to Ambassador Jarring.

Fourth, negotiate without preconditions but within the framework and spirit of the United Nations cease-fire resolution of December 1967.

Fifth, require the phased withdrawal of Soviet military manpower along with any Israeli troop withdrawal.

The only way any settlement can possibly be reached is by an agreement between Israel and her neighbors. What the United States and the Soviet Union must do is convince these countries of the urgency and importance of reaching an agreement.

It is essential to world peace and security that the match not be lit—we must look to Israel, the United Arab Republic and its allies and to the Soviet Union to be sensible and recognize the responsibility they each have to arrive at a settlement.

The elements of a lasting peace must include:

First, an end of the state of belligerence by the Arab States.

Second, the acceptance and recognition of Israel by her Arab neighbors.

Third, secure and recognized borders.

Fourth, free and safeguarded access to the Suez Canal and international waters, including the Gulf of Aqaba and the Persian Gulf.

Fifth, international guarantees of borders in the peace settlement.

Sixth, the stationing of U.N. peace-keeping forces at critical and sensitive border areas.

It has been suggested that the United States and Soviet troops should constitute the peace force. On this we should be most cautious and skeptical.

In considering such a possibility we ought to appreciate that this could well mean the presence of Soviet troops in the United Arab Republic in the foreseeable future. It could also more directly involve the United States and the Soviet Union in the Middle East. It would provide the Soviet Union with an argument for legitimatizing Soviet military presence in the United Arab Republic.

# APPENDIX II
# A CHANCE TO HALT
# THE ARMS RACE NOW

THE UNITED STATES and the Soviet Union have resumed meetings in Vienna—a city where peace has been made, or broken, on many occasions in the past. We are meeting to continue the strategic arms limitation talks, designed to arrest the terrifying race in nuclear arms before it can reach a new and even more dangerous level.

Several of my colleagues—most recently the distinguished Senator from Illinois (Mr. PERCY)— have vocalized their concern and introduced proposals to facilitate negotiations in an attempt to reach a satisfactory arms control agreement with the Soviet Union.

I would like to contribute constructively to this discussion and submit a resolution in that regard, intended to serve as a guideline to the administration.

At stake in these negotiations is the power of

man to control his cwn fate—by placing firm limits on weapons that could lead to his self-destruction.

No other issue more meaningfully affects our chances for a peaceful world, and indeed for the survival of mankind. No other issue more deserves our attention here in the U.S. Senate, as the two superpowers, the United States and the Soviet Union, once again raise our hopes and fears about the nuclear arms race and its end.

For many years, I have taken part in the efforts to bring the arms race under control. For several years, I served as chairman of the Senate Subcommittee on Disarmament and Arms Control. During that period, I introduced and cosponored resolutions in the Senate which led to the Limited Nuclear Test-Ban Treaty; as Vice President of the United States, I worked for the acceptance of the Non-Proliferation Treaty; and as Vice President I signed Protocol II of the Treaty for the Latin American Nuclear Free Zone. And I have long supported the initiation and holding of these important strategic arms limitation talks.

During the past 2 years, while absent from public life, I had a further chance to study these problems, as student and teacher, and watched with approval the courageous efforts by Members of the Senate to free us all from the tyranny of the nuclear arms race. Now the effort here, in the Congress, must be renewed, and I intend to contribute as best I can to help insure that it is not in vain.

As I speak today, the arms race is continuing,

despite the SALT talks and our hopes for their success.

When these talks did finally begin in November 1969, they promised to be an incentive for restraint on the part of the two superpowers. But they became instead an excuse for each side to pile up arms and more arms—each justifying its action on the claim that it was strengthening its bargaining position; in other words, each country giving itself a new bargaining chip.

The arms race goes on, oblivious of the negotiators, of the hard demands of peace, and of the welfare of this Nation. While we continue to stockpile weapons, we are diverting valuable funds from the basic needs of our own country. It is our own people who are caught in the arms race and now we must ask ourselves what price we are paying for the catchall of sufficient security, as defined by this administration.

By conservative estimates, the total cost of Minuteman III—our most advanced ICBM—alone will be about 5.6 billion dollars, and another $5.1 billion at current prices for the Poseidon missile for our nuclear submarines. Estimates for our Safeguard program depend on what plan the administration follows. We could spend from roughly $12 billion for 12 sites to $200 billion for total ABM deployment. In welfare terms, the cost is phenomenal both in actual fiscal expenditures and human resources.

Then we must ask ourselves if these weapons

would give us more security even if we were to buy them all. It is my view that they do not.

We did not enter the SALT talks with any doubts about the continued hostility of the Soviet Union toward us. Instead, we entered them with knowledge of the greater risks if we failed to act, and from awareness of two hard facts:

First, there was nothing that either Russians or ourselves could do to the other, including a full-scale surprise attack, that would prevent the nation being attacked from causing the sure destruction of the attacker in return—destruction of his industry, his cities, his population, and his society itself. No matter how it might begin, a nuclear war between our two countries would be mutual suicide. There can be no victory for anyone—only the defeat of the whole human race.

Second, both the United States and the Soviet Union had crossed the threshold of another round of the arms race. We had hoped that this could be avoided. But even if talks on arms reductions have been under way, a whole new dimension of weapons is now in the process of being constructed and deployed. If unchecked, it would cost vast sums of money; it would be more deadly than we have ever known before; and it would be less stable than the situation we know today.

These facts should have impelled both the United States and the Soviet Union to seek an end to nuclear competition.

Today, I would like to report with some assurance that this new round of the SALT talks, or one in the near future, will bring the arms race under control.

Unfortunately, I cannot do so, because of the difficulties that continue to surround the whole subject of limiting arms.

I am therefore submitting a resolution which I send to the desk. It reads:

### Resolution Relating to Armaments Limitations

Whereas the Governments of the United States and the Union of Soviet Socialist Republics have both expressed a willingness to deescalate the arms race by entering into the Strategic Arms Limitation Talks (SALT) to consider the control of strategic weapons;

Whereas the Government of the Union of Soviet Socialist Republics has recently shown an interest in negotiating agreed limitations on anti-ballistic missile defense systems and has slowed its deployment of ICBM's;

Whereas there is a strategic, political, and economic interrelationship between anti-ballistic missiles and multiple independently targeted re-entry vehicles (MIRV's); and whereas the regulation of both of these weapons systems could contribute to a halt in the arms race;

Whereas an agreement limiting ABM deployment would contribute to the negotiation of limitations on offensive strategic systems because it would reduce the need for new offensive weapons to maintain the deterrent;

Now therefore, be it Resolved, That as the first step toward achieving a more comprehensive agreement on both defensive and offensive weapons, the Senate request the President to propose at the negotiations with the Government of the Union of Soviet Socialist Republics for the purpose of entering into an agreement—

SEC. 1: 1. to ban or limit to a very low level the deployment of anti-ballistic missile systems by the Government of the United States and the Government of the Union of Soviet Socialist Republics;

2. to bind those Governments to conduct further negotiations to achieve a limitation on offensive strategic weapons;

The Senate also calls upon the President

SEC. 2: 1. to propose that the United States and the Union of Soviet Socialist Republics enter into a mutual freeze on the testing of multiple independently targeted re-entry vehicles and on the deployment of both offensive and defensive nuclear weapons, including anti-ballistic missiles and multiple independently targeted re-entry vehicles, for the duration of these negotiations with the understanding that the continued observance of the freeze requires comparable self-restraint by both parties.

2. to inform the Congress fully and promptly of all developments in the arms race which could affect the Strategic Arms Limitation Talks (SALT), and to consult regularly with the Senate on those developments.

We in the United States are handicapped by the unwillingness of the Soviet Union so far to make definite declarations of restraint concerning its own nuclear weapons programs.

As ever, the Russians remain silent about what they intend to do. At the SALT talks they have not been forthcoming on the U.S. proposal for a comprehensive agreement—an agreement covering both offensive and defensive nuclear arms.

Second, the Soviet Union appears to be resuming the deployment of land-based missiles, after a period of suspension lasting several months. This merely refuels the fires of suspicion and tension. We have heard a great deal in our press and through the media about this lately.

We are not yet sure what these new deployments entail, but it does appear that our hopes for a continuing moratorium on Soviet land-based missile deployments have not been realized.

At the same time, however, these difficulties must be set against two positive developments of the past few months.

The Soviet Union has not resumed work—and I repeat, has not resumed work—on a number of missile sites already under construction. These include the giant SS-9's.

In addition, the Russians have now shown a willingness to negotiate an agreement to limit antiballistic missile defenses. This, too, may indicate Soviet interest in finding a new way to regulate the nuclear relations between our two countries.

I believe that these two developments could be more important than other Soviet behavior and therefore, respectfully urge that the administration probe more deeply into them.

Regrettably, it appears that this administration has, instead, concentrated on inconclusive evidence that the Russians are continuing and expanding their nuclear missile program. Thus we become prisoners of our own fears, and fail to give due recognition to the possibilities that may be before us.

Surely we ought to have been seriously exploring and asking:

Why they suspended their deployment programs of the SS-9. Were they demonstrating restraint? Or were they merely pausing, before new efforts to increase the power and effectiveness of their land-based arsenal? We may never know. We made it difficult to test Russian motives because of our own stepped-up deployment program.

But we did not need to know what Soviet motives were. We could have responded with our own acts of restraint. And our risks would have been minimal compared to the gains we might have achieved.

In talking about arms control we must be prepared to take what I call minimal, prudent risks for peace, to try to slow down the arms race. This is the best way I know to promote both our national security and world peace.

As I said, we did not need to know what Soviet motives were. We could have responded with our own acts of restraint. There is precedent for this assertion. Both Presidents Eisenhower and Kennedy took unilateral action to stop our own nuclear testing; both acted in anticipation of a commensurate response from the Soviet Union and both were willing to accept less at the time than a complete test ban.

This is why we call it the limited nuclear test ban treaty. We can still exercise restraint today in ways that were long urged on the administration before the Russians launched their land-based missile program—if that is indeed what they are doing— and as yet we have no positive evidence that they are resuming this program.

We must not be panicked by recent Soviet moves, or headlines about them, into believing that all chances for ending the arms race are dead. They are not; they have become even more imperative; and they require even more restraint on both sides.

Restraint should begin with the weapons that

raise the most serious problems of immediate concern for the stability of the arms balance: The Soviet and our anti-ballistic-missile system, Soviet offensive missiles, and multiple independently targeted reentry vehicles—MIRV—both ours and theirs.

Our Safeguard system is presently deployed at three sites—and, if the administration has its way, it will be deployed at a fourth site, either in Wyoming or right here around Washington. So far this ABM is designed primarily to afford some protection for our land-based missile and bomber forces against a successful first-strike by the Soviet Union.

But this purpose has always been suspect: Few scientists really believe that Safeguard could thwart the attack of a determined aggressor. In any event, we have alternatives to Minuteman in order to deter a Soviet attack. Those alternatives include our bomber fleet and nuclear submarines with Polaris and Poseidon missiles. Come what may, we know and they know we can retaliate against any attack, at any time, from any quarter—with total devastating effect.

The arguments for Safeguard were always weak. Despite reported recent developments, they remain weak.

During a period of several months, the Soviet Union halted programs which, had they been continued unabated for long enough, and without any action by us, could have posed the threat of a disarming first-strike against Minuteman. According to Department of Defense figures in the posture statement, for 1971, the Soviet SS-9`program has leveled off at fewer than 300 missiles. Yet in order to launch an all-out first-strike against Minuteman, the Soviet Union would need at least 420 SS-9's, each armed with a MIRV system capable of bringing three separate targets under attack in order to implement this strategy. They do not have this MIRV system at this time.

I am aware, of course, that the Soviet Union could try to achieve this same purpose—the ability to launch a disarming attack against Minuteman—without increasing the total number of its SS-9's. It could install an advanced system of highly accurate MIRV's. Each would have to carry at least six separate warheads.

Today, we know that the Soviet Union has tested a simple, unguided, multiple warhead that could fire three warheads like a shotgun. The Russians may also have begun testing a rudimentary MIRV, capable of taking three separate targets under attack at one time. But they have clearly not finished the test program that would be necessary to develop their MIRV into a system capable of successfully attacking Minuteman Missiles in their hardened silos. Even more, there is no evidence that they have begun a test program for a MIRV with six warheads, despite all the suppositions and scare talk that appears from time to time.

Before the Russians could possibly deploy a system of offensive weapons capable of threatening our Minuteman force, they would have to make considerable strides, in their missile programs—particularly in the development of their MIRV.

Do the Russians intend to build a first-strike capability sufficient to destroy our Minuteman force?

I believe that this possibility is too fanciful to merit our serious concern.

It ignores the political developments of a decade in our relations with the Soviet Union.

It ignores the certainty that the Russians would face a continued, all-out nuclear arms race with us—a race they could not win. We would never stand idly by and permit that.

But most important, the case for believing in a Soviet first-strike capability against Minuteman ignores totally the existence of our powerful Polaris submarine force.

Today that force on its own—and without MIRV—is capable of utterly destroying the Soviet Union, if this brings any comfort to anyone. I sometime wonder about how mad we are. We talk about total destruction as if it were a game.

Indeed, if there were ever a real threat to our Nation that required the deployment of Poseidon submarines, one single Poseidon equipped submarine would be able to destroy a significant portion of the Soviet Union—one Poseidon could destroy 160 different cities.

We must understand one thing: we cannot continue to assert, without convincing evidence, that the Soviet Union is bent upon the destruction of our land-based missiles; and we must not undertake programs based upon that assertion. If we do, we stand to forfeit the possibility that the arms race itself can be brought to an end. Overinsurance, and the hysteria which breeds it, may only help to bring into being the very offensive threat that is the object of the Safeguard defense.

For these reasons, I call upon the President to propose a mutual freeze with the Soviet Union on ABM deployments, as an important first step in limiting both offensive and defensive arms. And the United States for its part should maintain this freeze for as long as the Soviet Union exercizes comparable self-restraint and refrains from taking action directed to counter the ability of the United States to respond effectively to a Soviet nuclear attack.

I believe we should take the initiative, just as President Kennedy and President Eisenhower did on two other occasions when they took the initiative unilaterally. This is not an awful risk, but it does represent leadership. We can take that leadership at this time because, as I speak to the Senate today, we do have massive retaliatory power. We do have a great deal of deterrent force. We do have a powerful strike force not only in our land-based missiles and bombers, but also in the Polaris fleet which in itself is a deterrent force, a strike force that the Soviet Union cannot counter.

This kind of mutual suspension which I am now

proposing could be policed through the satellite reconnaissance systems of each side.

The Soviet Union might not accept this mutual suspension. But at least we in the United States would be making an effort to stop the arms race— an effort which the Senate urged upon the administration last year, when the arms race was much less advanced. At that time, the President refused to act. We must not make the same mistake this year.

What about offensive weapons?

If we wish to bring the arms race to an end, it is essential that both superpowers exercise restraint in these weapons as well. For the United States it means halting the deployment of MIRV's. For the Soviet Union it means continuing its suspension of SS-9 deployments and refraining from deploying comparably large intercontinental ballistic missiles as well as from further testing of their own MIRV.

MIRV's are already being deployed on our Minuteman III missiles, and we will shortly be sending to sea the first of our Poseidon submarines.

Why did we develop this MIRV warhead in the first place, and begin to deploy it? The last two administrations have adopted these reasons—and I am quite familiar with at least one of those administrations.

First, the MIRV program was designed as a counter to a Soviet anti-ballistic-missile system which some people said might threaten our ability to counter-attack following a nuclear attack on us. Against such a Russian ABM system, MIRV would

enable us to maintain deterrence by guaranteeing
that enough warheads could always penetrate Soviet defenses, regardless of their ABM's.

But the Soviet Union has not built the ABM
system we feared. A few years ago the Senate was
filled with talk about what the Russians were going
to do with their ABM system; the fact is they have
not done anything with it—and the limited, already
outdated system they have deployed is not capable
of stopping an American retaliatory attack with our
existing arsenal—much less of stopping a MIRV
attack.

An effective ABM system would take the Russians many years, if not decades, to build; would be
incredibly expensive—and might not work in any
event.

Furthermore, if the Russians begin this ABM
system, we will know it immediately, through our
own reconnaissance satellites that give us positive
and reliable evidence of Soviet acts. An ABM system
requires very large pieces of equipment, radar equipment, and all of which is visible by use of reconnaissance satellites.

We could counter their efforts by deploying
MIRV warheads at a moment's call.

It is beyond dispute that we are far advanced
with MIRV technology—so far advanced that we
are already deploying the counter to a future Soviet ABM system. We have, in other words, considerable leadtime over the Soviets.

One fact should now be clear to anyone who

has looked at the awful logic of an arms race: If we build the counter to a weapon before that weapon is built, we will only inspire the other side to fulfill our worst fears. Yet this is exactly the course we seem to be pursuing.

There is a second reason advanced by the administration for building MIRV: to provide added insurance that we could retaliate following an attempt by the Soviet Union to destroy our bombers and land-based missiles in a surprise disarming attack. But with more targetable warheads, fewer missiles would have to survive in order to rain unacceptable damage in retaliation upon the Soviet Union.

And here, too, we can wait to deploy MIRV warheads to counter the potential threat—we can wait until we have evidence that the Soviets are expanding their offensive and defensive strategic nuclear arsenal where it poses a real threat to our ability to retaliate.

What I am asking for is that we do not chase each other in this costly, dangerous arms race. We are setting up assumptions and then we build weapons to meet the assumptions, only to precipitate the building of other weapons by the Soviet Union. And they do the same.

By deploying MIRV's now, we may attain a self-fulfilling prophecy by forcing the Soviet Union to accelerate its own land-based missile program or even to deploy another, more complete ABM system.

But a mutual freeze on ABM's would, on the other hand, remove a large part of the rationale for the existence of MIRV's. For these reasons, I believe that we should suspend further deployment of ABM's and MIRV's—in other words, either a freeze or agreement.

In addition, I believe Congress should act to place in escrow all funds for MIRV deployment.

If we should have reason to believe that the Soviet Union is not responding with similar restraint —in other words, that it does not take commensurate action—then this Congress and our President must, of course, do what would appear to be necessary.

But if we were to put in escrow the funds for the deployment of MIRV, Congress could continue to appropriate the funds needed for a MIRV program; and the Russians would not doubt our resolve to resume this program if their actions made it necessary.

By putting the funds in escrow, we would be taking a positive step to exercise restraint in the arms race.

At the same time, I propose that the administration require the Soviet Union to match our restraint by suspending, once again, their land-based missile programs and MIRV testing. We should expect that our restraint in halting deployment and testing of MIRV's will evoke a comparable response from the Soviet Union.

People are going to say, "You will never get it

done this way, Senator." I submit that we have to try. I think we have to be as ingenious at the peace table as we can be at the arsenal and in the field. I think we have to develop peace weapons and peace technologies, just as we have developed military weapons and technologies. We have spent billions of dollars on weapons technologies. We must use every bit of ingenuity and inventive genius in the intellectual and diplomatic realm that we have, to probe and to search for ways and means of slowing down this arms race without in any way sacrificing our own security.

I have been in Congress long enough, and have served in high office long enough, to be concerned about our security. My point is that we are not gaining any more security. What we are getting today is less security and less stability. What we are getting today is a costly, dangerous, deadly arms race.

There are still further reasons for us to withhold deployment of MIRV warheads. What will happen if we fail to do so? The answer becomes clear after a careful reading of President Nixon's foreign policy report this year.

In his report, the President said that our MIRV's would contribute to the stability of the arms race, but that Russian MIRV's, if they are developed and deployed, would be destabilizing.

He cannot have it both ways. Listen to the remarks of the President:

Deployed in sufficient numbers and armed with (MIRV's) of sufficient accuracy (the SS-9) could threaten our land-based ICBM forces. Our MIRV systems, by contrast do not have the combination of numbers accuracy and warhead yield to pose a threat to the Soviet land-based ICBM force.

I guess it depends on which end of the telescope you are looking through. Whom do we think we are kidding? Are we building a nuclear force for a Fourth of July celebration? Is that what this is all about? Has our nuclear force suddenly become a little social enterprise?

Why should the Russians believe us when we try to reassure them about our MIRV's, when we distrust them about theirs? And why should we assume that the Russians will believe that a weapon we are deploying will pose less of a threat than a weapon which the Soviet Union has not yet even adequately tested?

For many years the arms race has continued unabated because each of us, the United States and the Soviet Union, has insisted on a double standard. We in this country have argued that we would never start a nuclear war—and I am sure we will not—and we know this to be true. This, in our minds, has justified our having a superiority or sufficiency of nuclear firepower.

At the same time, the Russians argued and

acted on the basis of Communist doctrine that the capitalist West would start the last great war. In other words, the Soviets have rationalized and justified their nuclear arsenal on the basis of their defense.

We may reject their doctrine, but we must not fail to understand the result of this parallel process of belief: each of us continues to rush ahead in the arms race, convinced that the other is the real villain.

Neither of us can any longer indulge ourselves in this practice of placing all the blame for the nuclear arms race on the other.

We in the United States, therefore, cannot argue that our MIRV's are weapons for peace, and theirs are weapons for war. Nor can they. We must realize that we are trapped together in this mad circle of escalation, and must work together to break out of it.

Of course, it is widely argued that it is too late to head off a competition in these MIRV warheads.

We are told that yet another genie is out of the bottle, and that the Soviet Union will inevitably respond, and may even be doing so now, to our MIRV deployments, with new nuclear deployments of their own—one day including MIRV's.

For those of us who long ago urged the postponement of our MIRV program for this very reason—and who now watch new Soviet activity in land-based missiles—it is cold comfort to be told now that we were right.

I do not believe that it is too late to act.

Perhaps the Russians will undertake a full program to test MIRV's, and deploy them in significant numbers.

Perhaps.

But we will never know whether they can be convinced not to deploy MIRV's—and possibly a new ABM system, as well if we rush ahead with our own MIRV program. In despair, we would make our prophecy self-fulfilling.

There is one further reason for suspending deployment of our MIRV's at this time. Part of the nuclear equation is closely related to the total number of nuclear warheads and firepower on each side.

The President has dealt with this issue in defining his concept of nuclear sufficiency. According to this concept, we must have enough power to prevent our being blackmailed by the Soviet Union. Therefore, as the President has said:

Our strategic power (must) not be inferior to that of any other state.

I heartily concur.

For that reason, we must be watchful concerning any new activity in the Soviet strategic nuclear missile programs.

But I also recognize that the Russians claim this prerogative and would resist the right of a foreign power to exercize nuclear blackmail over them. They, too, must be concerned with the number of our warheads—as it increases radically with our deployment of MIRV.

This is why over the years both sides have come to accept that neither must be allowed to become so superior to the other as to make it vulnerable to political blackmail.

President Nixon endorsed this concept in his press conference on March 4.

And as long ago as March 7, 1970, the Soviet Union endorsed parity—and claimed it for itself—in an article which appeared in Pravda, the most authoritative public source of Soviet thinking:

> The military strategic balance of forces existing in the world makes quite unrealistic any of the West's militarist circles' calculations about the possibility of winning in the event of a thermonuclear war, and judging from everything, a new spiral in the arms race could not change the essence of this balance.

And it noted even further that:

> At the basis of the Soviet approach to the problem of restricting strategic arms there is no desire to receive any additional unilateral advantages for itself in the sphere of safeguarding just its security alone.

I do not suggest that we in the United States should permit the Soviet Union to be roughly equal with us in nuclear power out of any abstract notions of nuclear justice.

Quite the contrary: We must accept this kind of equality as the only basis for stability, and the point at which arms control can begin.

We are dealing with a psychological concept—that each nation feels equal, and can permit a lowering of political tensions, whatever may be the true facts of the case. Indeed, the Russians claimed equality with us—and endorsed an end to the arms race—at a time when they were markedly and demonstrably inferior to us in every form of nuclear power except land-based missiles.

But if the Russians can be comfortable with that situation, and can urge that the competition come to an end, then it would be foolish for us to make their inferiority even more apparent, and force them to take a new hard look at their position relative to us.

These questions of restraint on ABM and MIRV are doubly important at this very moment. At the end of this month, the 24th Congress of the Soviet Communist Party will be convened.

High on the agenda will be the issue of East-West relations.

Efforts will be made by the Soviet military leaders to portray the United States as an aggressive power, bent on the destruction of the Soviet Union. We will present them with a set of most persuasive arguments if they can demonstrate that we are continuing the arms race at a faster rate than they are.

The Soviet Union is clearly not a pluralistic society in the sense that we know pluralism.

The Russians have some tough hardline militarists in their Government.

But there are people in the Soviet society and Government who are concerned about both the risks and costs of the arms race, just as we are.

There are strong incentives for the Soviet Union, as well as for the United States, to change its priorities away from an arms race that costs them far more relative to the rest of the economy than it does us.

We can help make that possible, by not undermining those people in the Soviet Union who share our objective of slowing down the arms race.

I suggest that we try to appeal to the men of reason.

By suspending the deployment of our MIRV's, coupled with an offer to freeze our ABM position, we could strengthen our hand at the SALT talks. SALT talks have resumed in Vienna, and what happens in them will depend more on what the superpowers do with their own weapons programs than what they say in Vienna.

Last year, we were told that we must continue work on an ABM system as a "bargaining chip" to be used in those negotiations.

Whatever the merits of that view, we should realize that we now have that chip—and the one represented by our capability to deploy MIRV's at will.

But we are in danger of changing our bargaining chip into a chip on our shoulder, if we do not show restraint.

It is one thing to prepare ourselves to continue programs if the Soviet Union does not negotiate in earnest; it is quite another thing to build so many arms that the Soviet Union will have no alternative but to respond in kind, and even to suspend productive work at SALT while they try, once again, to catch up with us.

Indeed, the reputed Soviet resumption of a land-based missile program may be no more than an attempt to play our game: To reestablish a bargaining chip of their own, and another chip on their shoulder.

As Admiral Moorer has said:

There is an interaction between what we do and what the Soviets do.

A demonstration of restraint is an essential preliminary step in the process of building the climate needed for success at SALT.

But there are steps that we can take during the negotiations themselves.

I recognize that we all must be very careful here. The President, as Commander in Chief, is primarily responsible for our security. He, alone, must make the final decision on our negotiation posture at the strategic arms limitation talks.

But the Senate also has a role to play, above and beyond its power to give our "advice and consent" to the President on a specific treaty. As a coordinate branch of the Government, Congress at all times has joint responsibility with the President for deciding our military posture, and has the power of the purse strings to insure that it plays an active part in making security policy for our Nation.

It would be folly to believe that the Senate should only be consulted when a treaty is presented to it. We have the experience with the Treaty of Versailles to chasten us. Then President Wilson's failure to consult adequately with Members of the Senate who opposed him but were open to persuasion doomed that treaty from the start, and helped set us on the road to World War II.

The same can be said of the Southeast Asian experience, when Congress and the public suffered from inadequate consultation which bred a feeling of distrust between the two branches of Government and damaged our policies at home and abroad.

In dealing with problems of nuclear strategy and arms control, we cannot afford to repeat these practices. The President must take the Senate into his confidence every step of the way.

Last year, the President requested funds for phase II of Safeguard, and the Senate complied after lengthy debate. Yet we know now that for some months, the Soviet Union had slowed down its SS-9 program. Had the President been more forthcoming about this information, the Senate's deliberations may have proceeded differently.

This year, therefore, it is incumbent upon the Senate to fulfill the responsibilities it has under the Constitution.

We have this responsibility in the conduct of the SALT talks.

Without attempting to bind the President to any set course of action, therefore, we owe him our support and allegiance in declaring our own position on the best way to proceed to SALT.

In this regard, we have to note the major shift in Soviet policy during the past year: I repeat, the willingness of the Soviet Union to consider an agreement on antiballistic missiles alone.

While being duly cautious in assessing Soviet motives, we must not underestimate the significance of this development. It represents a declaration by Moscow of the need to halt one area of the nuclear arms race, and a new road to travel.

An agreement to ban or limit to a very low level any further ABM deployment would not be the end of that road, but only a station on the way. Nor would we limit our own actions by agreeing, as the first step, to stop this part of the nuclear competition. We could—and we should—hold an ABM agreement to be only the first important part of a more comprehensive agreement, to be negotiated as soon as possible following the first step. We would not halt our research and development of an ABM system; nor would we sign without an escape clause that would permit us to abrogate the agreement if the Soviet Union pursued programs that violated the agreement or limited the ability of the United States to respond to a Soviet nuclear attack. And, if need be, we could place a time limit on the agreement, to require further, negotiated progress in other parts of the arms race. There are many alternatives. I am merely asking that we try to see whether they apply.

Our objective must be an agreement, formal or tacit, on both offensive and defensive strategic nuclear weapons. The President insists that such a comprehensive agreement be concluded at one time.

This approach has not yet proved successful in making a breakthrough toward an agreement of any kind. I maintain that an ABM agreement could and should be explicitly linked to an agreement on offensive weapons. In fact, I would suggest that an ABM ban is the essential first step.

Critics will say that the first step will be the last, that the Soviet Union will have no incentive to negotiate further agreements if they once could neutralize our Safeguard system. I do not believe this. I believe that any agreement with the Soviet Union on these matters—or any tacit actions of restraint will build toward others. Together, these steps could eventually bring an end to the entire race in nuclear arms. In

1963, we negotiated a halt to the testing of nuclear weapons on the ground, under water, and in the air. That limited test ban treaty was never considered the last act in arms control; rather, it has helped to build the climate which we now find supporting our efforts to take more substantial steps. In fact, that agreement was step No. 1 toward the so-called Nonproliferation Treaty, which was step No. 2.

So, too, an agreement on ABM's alone will not release either of our two countries from the solemn pledge we have made to stop our race in every nuclear arm. We made this pledge in the Nonproliferation Treaty, not out of altruism, but out of a hardheaded recognition that we could not expect other nations to exercise nuclear restraint—by not building their first bomb—unless both the superpowers began work to end their race in more deadly weapons. Article VI required the parties to "pursue negotiations in good faith on effective measures relating to cessation of the nuclear arms race at an early date." It is under that article that we are proceeding with the SALT talks.

And the NPT will continue to succeed only as long as the SALT talks themselves show progress—or there is other evidence of superpower restraint, such as the suspension of programs that I have proposed.

The SALT talks must continue; and they must lead to a conclusion that all the world can see, and that will discharge the responsibilities that are expected of the mightiest nations of the world. The superpowers do have a responsibility for peace and for promoting the conditions that are conducive to peace.

But most important, the SALT talks are a forum for protecting our national self-interest. They will continue only as far and as fast as both superpowers recognize that it is in their self-interest to proceed. What comes first is of lesser importance. If we negotiate an end to deployment of the ABM, the Soviet Union will not lose its incentive to bring the rest of the arms race to an end, nor will we. The perils of an offensive nuclear arms race will remain the same; the economic incentive to desist will be just as strong. And the Soviet Union will be no more likely to acquire a nuclear capability that would permit it to launch a first-strike against us, or to hold us to ransom through a large increase in offensive arms.

Therefore, I strongly urge the President to begin this round of the SALT talks by negotiating a ban or at least a low-limit level on the ABM. He has himself said that we can only expect to succeed at SALT by being flexible in the way we approach these talks. The President also has stated that:

> We will negotiate an agreement that is not comprehensive but it must include offensive as well as defensive weapons, some mix.

We do not reject the need for an agreement on both offensive and defensive missiles. I surely do not. We merely move toward that objective step by step—each carefully measured. This is the pattern of United States-Soviet relations. And, we have made progress by following this course.

I do not speak in theory. I speak from the record of history. In the past 9 years, we have seen total disarmament in Antarctica; a nuclear test ban undersea, in the atmosphere, and on the ground; an atomic quarantine for Latin America; a nuclear non-proliferation treaty to curb the spread of weapons and technology; a treaty banning the use of nuclear weapons in outer space and, most recently, a treaty barring nuclear weapons and launching installations from the ocean seabed.

We have made progress negotiating with the Soviet Union. It is not as if they were a wall of granite, obstinate, stupid, stubborn to the point of doing nothing. If we pursue our program for peace with prudence and tenacity, we can make progress. In fact, we must.

In the past 2 years, both the Russians and ourselves have repeatedly declared our desire to slow down the arms race; yet the piling up of arms continues. The two nuclear giants have recognized their mutual self-interest, yet they have been powerless to put it into effect.

This is what was meant when we talked of the "mad momentum" of the arms race. It is mad—insane—to persist in this folly.

Of course, an agreement at SALT must reflect

patience, understanding, and mutual accommodation. But we must not forget that every day we waste on finding the proper formula for halting the arms race, either by agreement or by concrete acts, we move one more day along in massing of weapons and passing of new thresholds.

I submit to the Senate that there are massive, new weapons systems on the drawing board in the Pentagon and, I am sure, in the Soviet pentagon as well. We can bankrupt ourselves and get no more security.

Bureaucrats on both sides have become paralyzed; misplaced caution betokens a far greater recklessness; and we both insure that an end to the arms race, if it ever does come, will be at a far higher level of weaponry than was true 2 years ago, or is true even now.

For too long, we have allowed ourselves to think that the arms race was a technical problem requiring technical solutions. Now we have learned two lessons:

First, the strategy of deterrence is as much a matter of psychology as of military weapons.

Second, and even more important, controlling the arms race is a political problem, requiring political solutions. It cannot be accomplished by experts, by the military, or by technicians. Experts should be on tap, not on top. There are political decisions which have to be made. Stopping the arms race can only be done by leaders responsible for the overall well-being of their people, and who have a sufficient grasp of history and of men to end the tyranny of nuclear technology and our cowardice before it.

I believe that it is time for both sides to act to end the arms race—now. That is why I propose this resolution today.

We have an opportunity today to slow the whole race down. And we must take it. We have taken many risks on the battlefield—in Vietnam, Laos, Cambodia—at the direction of Presidents. It is now time, and the situation demands, that we take some risks for peace and security.

It is also time to recognize the tremendous economic costs of the nuclear arms race, and the waste that it represents for us in America in terms of our domestic needs. Of course, throughout our history, we have believed that nothing could stand in the way of our own security—that no cost was too great to insure our future peace of mind.

There is no such question today—our security is guaranteed, and a failure to halt the arms race will even make us less secure.

It is proper, therefore, to question the diversion of needed resources to strategic nuclear programs which were once so crucial to us, but which now may produce more threat to us than safety.

The strength of our Nation is made up of many factors. We have accounted for the factor of nuclear might. Now we must be concerned with our domestic strength, as well—with our cities, housing, education, health, poverty, the environment. These are needs we will never meet—strength that we will never build—if we persist in placing unlimited funds in nuclear weapons programs that add nothing to our security.

I speak at a moment of unique promise—and peril. For the first time in more than 20 years, we see the possibility of bringing some order into Soviet-American competition in nuclear weapons, leading to a day when these weapons will not loom so large in our relations. It is a promise for everyone—that all the world can rest more easily in the knowledge that the two great custodians of this destructive power could recognize their own self-interest in stopping the arms race, and recognize their responsibilities to all mankind.

But there is peril in our present course of action. By placing too much weight on detail—too much weight on remote threats—too much weight on suspicion—that appears only on the far reaches of our imagination—we may squander the opportunity that is ours today. This is no time for timidity, or for blind obedience to outdated doctrines of building every weapon it is possible to have. Our back is laden, burdened with the weight of these weapons.

This is a time for trust—not of Soviet intentions —but of ourselves. Trust that our undoubted strength can be used as a base for building a better world. Trust that we can find a way through the difficult and uncertain days ahead, as we negotiate an end to the arms race. And trust that our efforts can give us that future—secure and safe—that is ours to have.

The future of the world itself may very well depend upon our confidence in ourselves and our trust in ourselves.

I hope that this message today will make some contribution to a most complex and difficult assignment.

I recognize that the President has an exceedingly difficult task in the negotiations at Vienna.

I did not make this speech to enter into a debate with the President. I made it as a contribution to the thinking of ways and means to bring about deescalation in the arms race, and effective control over weapons of mass destruction.

I appeal to the leaders of our Government to be ingenious. I appeal to them to be tenacious. I appeal to them to have faith in ourselves and our capacity to give leadership to the world.

As we are now in a program, hopefully, of withdrawal from Southeast Asia, may we be able to forge a program of leadership in the cause of world peace. There can be no peace in the world if the arms race continues unending and unabated.

The beginning of peace is in the mind of man.

The mind of man must find a way through political decision, through negotiation and diplomacy, to bring a halt to the arms race which consumes our resources and threatens our very lives, and which gives us little or no security or stability.